A NEW APPROACH
TO Sight Singing

A NEW APPROACH TO
Sight Singing

SOL BERKOWITZ, *Assistant Professor of Music*
GABRIEL FONTRIER, *Assistant Professor of Music*
LEO KRAFT, *Assistant Professor of Music*
Queens College of the City of New York

W · W · NORTON & COMPANY · INC · *New York*

Library of Congress Catalog Card No. 60-5697

ISBN 0 393 09538 X

PRINTED IN THE UNITED STATES OF AMERICA

67890

To John Edward Castellini,
our teacher, our good friend and colleague, our editor,
this book is affectionately dedicated.

Contents

Acknowledgements

It is a pleasure to acknowledge the wholehearted help and encouragement given to us, during the period in which this book was written, by our colleagues in the Queens College Music Department. Their suggestions were most stimulating and useful.

We are especially indebted to Professor John Castellini, our patient and devoted editor, who continually labored with our manuscript and helped define its final form. We gratefully thank Professor Saul Novack of the Music Department for his constructive help and advice, and Dr. Joseph Raben of the English Department for his careful reading of the prose in this book.

Many of our basic ideas concerning music and music theory were gained during our years as students and colleagues of the late Karol Rathaus. To him, then, we owe a special debt of gratitude.

And, since this book grew out of our classroom experience, we sincerely thank the many gifted and industrious students in our classes whose eagerness to learn led us to better understanding of what might prove most useful in A New Approach to Sight Singing.

SOL BERKOWITZ
GABRIEL FONTRIER
LEO KRAFT

Queens College,
January, 1960

Preface

This book consists of a coordinated body of musical material *specifically composed* for the study of sight singing.

A mastery of the art of singing at sight is essential to the instrumentalist, the singer, the musicologist, indeed to any musician or intelligent amateur. Ideally, the young student should be taught this skill from the moment his vocal or instrumental instruction begins, but actually very few music students enjoy the benefits of such early training. Far too many reach an advanced level of instruction with little ability in sight singing, and this is often true even of students whose instrumental or vocal equipment is of professional concert caliber. Courses in sight singing, therefore, are a necessary part of the music curriculum of secondary schools, conservatories, colleges, and universities.

A number of textbooks have been published for use in sight-singing courses, which make use of excerpts from vocal and instrumental literature. The present volume, however, consists entirely of music especially composed for the study of sight singing. In more than a decade of teaching sight singing at Queens College of the City of New York, the authors have written a considerable number of melodies and duets for classroom use. They found that they were able to strike a particular level of difficulty and focus upon specific problems more effectively by composing material to meet the students' needs than by using melodies drawn from standard literature. They have also tried to aid their students by devising exercises which could be practiced without the assistance of an instructor. This book includes drills of the type which have proved most useful. Thus, the entire book has grown out of classroom experience which has convinced the authors that material for the study of sight singing should be written especially for that purpose.

A New Approach to Sight Singing contains five chapters and supplementary exercises. The first chapter contains melodies; the second, sets of variations; the third, duets; the fourth, accompanied melodies; the fifth, studies in vocal improvisation. The supplementary exercises consist of special drills. There is also a glossary in which foreign language music terms are defined.

Each chapter is divided into four sections, and the material in each section is graded in order of increasing difficulty. In every chapter, Section I consists of elementary material, Section II, intermediate, Sections III and IV, advanced. The unit of work is the section: Section I materials in each of the five chapters make up a coordinated body of music, and are intended to be used concurrently. The same applies to Sections II, III, and IV.

For example, students on the elementary level will begin with the first section of each of the chapters. A typical class hour might start with the singing of a group of melodies (Chapter One, Section I). One of the sets of variations (Chapter Two, Section I) might follow; the class could then turn to the duets (Chapter Three, Section I), the accompanied melodies (Chapter Four, Section I), or the improvisation studies (Chapter Five, Section I). It is not expected that all five chapters will be drawn upon in the course of any one hour. The bulk of class time will probably be devoted to the melodies, which comprise about one-half of the book. But the frequent use of Chapters Two, Three, Four, and Five will make possible a variety of approaches to the study of sight singing, and will also show the student how the skill which he acquires in any one area can be extended and applied to other musical situations.

A *New Approach to Sight Singing* is so organized that it may be adapted to either a two-semester or a four-semester course of study. Sections I and II, being essentially diatonic, may be integrated with the study of diatonic harmony; while Sections III and IV lend themselves to coordination with the study of chromatic harmony.

The *Melodies*, which constitute Chapter One, encompass a wide variety of musical styles and are graded progressively in terms of both technical and musical difficulty.

Section I, consisting of diatonic melodies, emphasizes the fundamental aspects of tonality. Stepwise motion, skips in simple contexts, and basic rhythmic patterns serve to introduce elementary problems of sight singing.

The melodies of Section II, while still diatonic, include simple modulations to the dominant or relative major, and gradually introduce more difficult rhythms.

Section III contains melodies with more elaborate modulations and chromatic embellishments, and introduces modal idioms. Phrase structures are more diverse, rhythms more complex.

In Section IV, the melodies include more challenging problems in tonality, rhythm and meter, phrase structure, dynamics, and musical interpretation.

The treble, alto, and bass clefs are used in all sections; the tenor clef is introduced in Section IV.

From one melody to the next the student will encounter changes of key, clef, rhythm, meter, tempo, dynamics, phrasing, and style. Grouping the melodies according to isolated technical characteristics has been deliberately avoided, for such an approach is arbitrary and unmusical. Rather, a more realistic approach is followed whereby the student is gradually introduced to the manifold problems he will face in practical musical situations. Moreover, within each level of difficulty there is a diversity of musical styles as well as technical problems.

Some melodies embody the expansive contour of the Baroque line; some demonstrate nineteenth-century chromaticism; others derive from folk and jazz idioms.

The *Themes and Variations,* Chapter Two, provide the experience of singing compositions of relatively extended duration, and also emphasize problems of musical interpretation. Because the character of the melodies changes from one variation to another, the student is helped to develop a sensitive performance technique.

Chapters Three, Four, and Five serve a twofold purpose. First, they stimulate the study of sight singing by approaching it from different points of view. Second, they present many different musical problems which demand varied applications of sight-singing technique.

The *Duets,* Chapter Three, have as their purpose the development of both independence and the sense of ensemble in part singing.

Chapter Four, which introduces the use of the piano, will help the student to increase his awareness of correct intonation. This chapter also encourages the discipline of a steady rhythm, and develops coordination between singing and playing. These *Play and Sing* exercises also point up the harmonic implications of a melodic line.

The *Improvisation Studies,* which comprise Chapter Five, add a new dimension to the study of sight singing. These studies are designed to help develop a good understanding of the relationship among melody, harmony, and rhythm. They require the student to look ahead, to "sight" before he sings, and to start thinking in terms of a complete musical phrase.

The *Supplementary Exercises* provide a variety of materials designed as drills in intervalic relationships, intonation, and rhythm. Part One of the *Supplementary Exercises* is designed for use with Sections I and II of the five chapters, while Part Two is to be used with Sections III and IV.

Everyone can learn to sing. Whether or not he possesses a

beautiful voice, anyone can achieve satisfactory sight singing ability by consistent study. Correct sight singing is a skill, a developed ability, and can be acquired only through diligent practice. The satisfaction gained in developing such an important skill will more than justify the hours devoted to the study of this discipline. Sight singing is certainly not an end in itself, but only one of many necessary skills which any intelligent musician must develop. Music does not live on paper. To bring it to life there must be an instrument that can sing, an ear that can hear, and a sensitive mind that can sing and hear in the silence of thought.

A NEW APPROACH
TO Sight Singing

CHAPTER
ONE
Melodies

Before singing a melody (or performing music of any sort)
it is necessary to understand thoroughly the system of
music notation we use today. The five-line staff, clef signs, time
signatures, tempo indications, and expression markings constitute a music code, all the elements of which must be decoded
simultaneously in order to transform into meaningful music
what has been set down on paper.

ESTABLISH THE KEY

The melodies in this chapter are tonal. Each is written in a
specific key and the student must establish that key before attempting to sing. The tonic note of the key (rather than the
first note of the melody) should be played on the piano or the
pitch pipe and sung by the student. Then the scale of the key
should be sung, ascending and descending, after which an
arpeggio consisting of tonic, third, fifth and octave may be
sung to establish further a feeling for the tonality of the melody.

ESTABLISH THE TEMPO

Next it is necessary to take cognizance of the tempo (rate of
speed) and the meter (number of beats to the measure). Many

15

different tempo indications have been used in this book to familiarize the student with most of the terms in common use. It is important that the singer know the meaning of these tempo markings, all of which are to be found in the Glossary (page 313).

The time signature denotes meter. Simple meters (duple, triple, and quadruple) are indicated by signatures having a 2, 3 or 4 as the upper numeral, or by the signs C (corresponding to $\frac{4}{4}$ meter) and ¢ (*alla breve*, corresponding to $\frac{2}{2}$ meter). Compound meters are combinations of simple meters within one measure.

Tempo can be established and meter defined by the student if he beats time as a conductor does. Standard conducting patterns should be used consistently. $\frac{6}{8}$ time may be conducted in six or in two beats; $\frac{9}{8}$ and $\frac{12}{8}$ time in separate beats or in three or four beats respectively. Tempo, and often the character of a melody, will serve the student in determining how to conduct compound meters.

SINGING MELODIES WITHOUT TEXTS

It is advisable to sing some definite syllable for every note the better to control quality and intonation. In many foreign countries *solfeggio* (the application of the *sol-fa* syllables to the degrees of the scale) is used in sight singing. This practice is officially sanctioned by foreign national conservatories. In our country, however, several methods of singing melodies without texts are in common use. These may be summarized as follows:

Fixed Do

In the fixed *Do* system, our notes, C, D, E, F, G, A, and B, are called *Do, Re, Mi, Fa, Sol, La,* and *Ti.* In singing a melody, the name for each note is sung without regard to any accidental. Countries which use this technique have been quite

successful with it, perhaps because of the rigorous early training which their students receive.

Movable Do

In the movable *Do* system, *Do* always represents the tonic or
first degree of the scale, regardless of key. Accidentals are ac-
counted for by changing the syllables. The ascending chromatic
scale reads as follows:

Do, Di, Re, Ri, Mi, Fa, Fi, Sol, Si, La, Li, Ti, Do

The descending chromatic scale reads as follows:

Do, Ti, Te, La, Le, Sol, Se, Fa, Mi, Me, Re, Ra, Do

When a melody modulates, the new tonic is called *Do*, and
the other notes of the scale are renamed accordingly. The purpose of this system is to emphasize the relationship between
the degrees of the scale, and to develop a feeling for tonality
even when the tonal center shifts.

Other Methods

Numbers (1, 2, 3) may be used instead of syllables (*Do, Re,
Mi*). The application is the same as in the movable *Do* system.
One syllable, such as *la,* may be used for all pitches. Thus
the singer does not have to translate the pitch names into syllables or numbers.

A musician is expected to know the system in common use
wherever he may be; therefore, the student should master more
than one of these techniques.

PHRASING

The student is urged to avoid note-to-note singing and to
make a genuine effort to grasp an entire phrase as a musical
unit. To guide and encourage this process of looking ahead,
slurs have been placed over the phrases of every melody. These
slurs define the phrase structure.

MUSICAL VALUES

In practicing the singing of melodies, as in practicing the piano or violin, the beginner may be tempted to concentrate his entire attention on producing the correct pitch, hoping that other musical values will be acquired in due course. But melodies have nuances of dynamics and tempo, contrasts, and climaxes, and these artistic qualities give meaning to the music. The student who wishes to improve his musicianship while learning the technique of sight singing must begin to think about musical values with the first melody in the book. As an aid to intelligent and sensitive performance we have included dynamics, expression, and articulation markings throughout the book. The eye should be trained to observe them; the mind to implement them.

Clearly, there is much to do, and it is suggested that the student *make haste slowly*. The first melodies should be studied carefully in order to develop good musical habits. The student should sing a melody several times, if necessary, until he can perform it with ease and fluency.

Melodies · SECTION I

Section I is to be used with Section I of all other chapters.

The first melodies emphasize the basic aspects of tonality.

They were designed to include easily recognizable scale and chordal patterns. These diatonic melodies are based upon both major and minor modes.

The phrases are usually symmetrical and short enough to be grasped at a glance. However, the diversity of keys, modes, tempos, dynamics, and clefs should provide a variety of musical experiences. The alto clef is introduced with #20; compound meter $\frac{6}{8}$ with #43; the minor mode with #72.

Students who are unfamiliar with one or another of the clefs that are used in this section should prepare for the actual singing by reciting the names of the notes in strict time. Then the melody should be sung, again naming the notes. To develop facility in reading the various clefs, the student should also *play* the melodies which have been sung in class.

19

Melodies · SECTION I

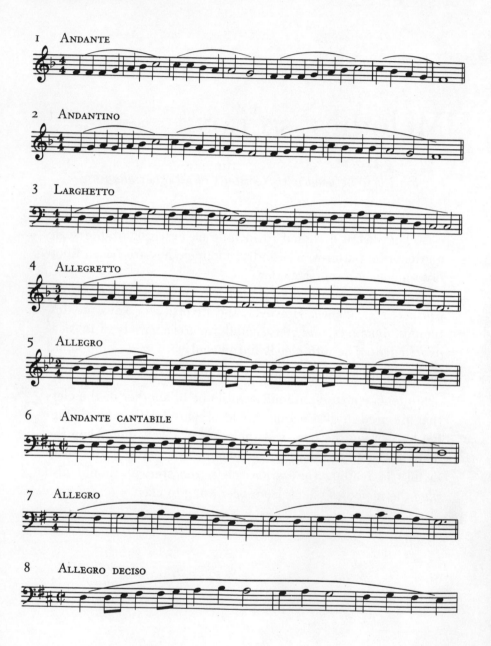

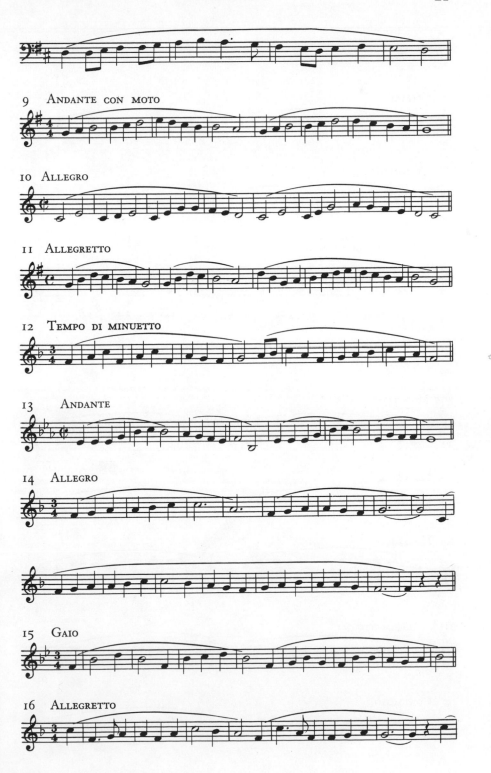

17 VIVACE

18 ANDANTE

19 ALLEGRO CON SPIRITO

The same melody in three clefs

20a MODERATO

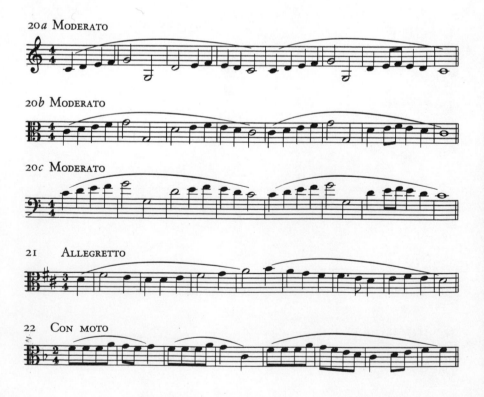

20b MODERATO

20c MODERATO

21 ALLEGRETTO

22 CON MOTO

63 Con moto

64 Ben ritmico

65 Allegro

66 Teneramente

71   Adagietto

The minor scales

Natural

Harmonic

Melodic

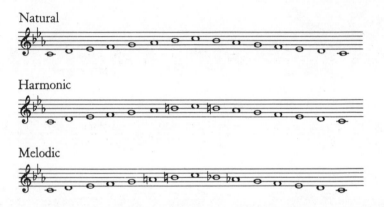

For a set of exercises comparing the major and minor modes, see Supplement, page

72   Adagietto

73   Andante sostenuto

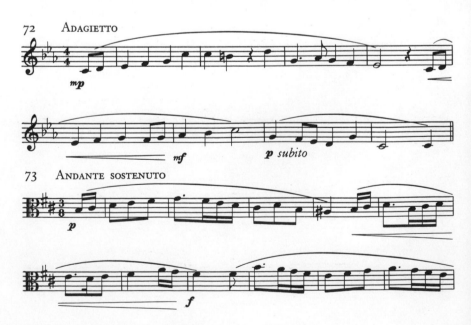

74 ANDANTINO

sotto voce

75 ANDANTE   Melody of Themes and Variations, #1

76 ALLEGRETTO

77 GIOCOSO

78 LARGHETTO

79 ALLEGRETTO

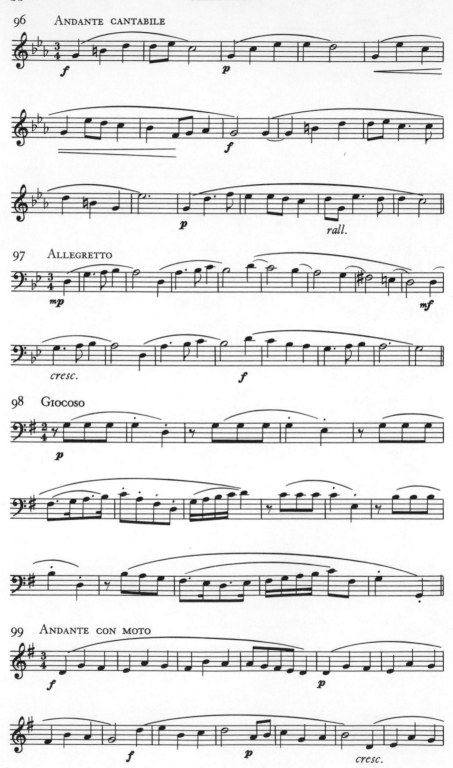

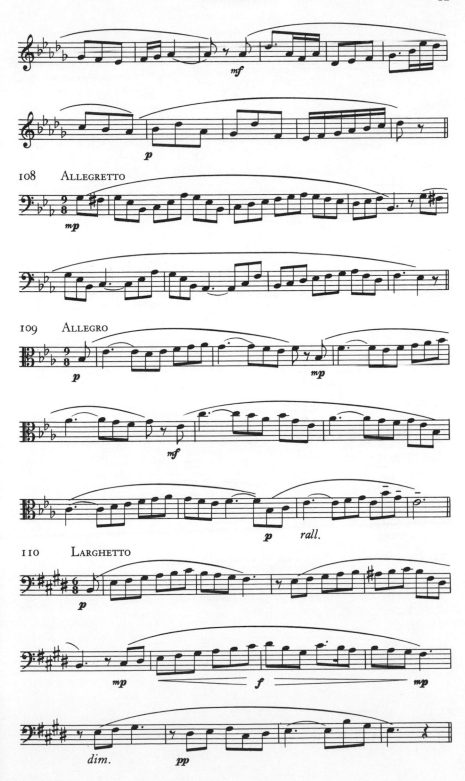

120 CON MOTO

121 ALLEGRO MODERATO   Var. V of Themes and Variations, #3

122 NICHT ZU SCHNELL

123 CON MOTO

128 ALLEGRO

129 ALLEGRETTO

130 ANDANTE

131 LIVELY

132 ANDANTE PASTORALE

133 MODERATO CON MOTO

134 ADAGIETTO

135 ALLEGRO

Melodies · SECTION II

Section II is to be used with Section II of all other chapters.

These melodies contain simple modulations, more complex rhythms, and diatonic skips in a variety of contexts. As in Melodies, Section I, the tonality of each melody is clearly defined. Some phrases are longer; some less symmetrical; syncopations are introduced; and the vocal range is extended.

Melodies · SECTION II

145 ANDANTINO

146 MODERATO

147 PRESTO

148 ALLEGRETTO GRAZIOSO

149 Assez animé

150 Allegro

Fine

Da Capo al Fine

151 Andantino

perdendosi

156 SWING IT

157 ALLEGRETTO

158 ANDANTE E MESTO

159 SCHERZO

cresc.

164 ZIEMLICH BEWEGT

165 ANDANTE GIOVALE

166 MARCH

Var. V of Themes and Variations, #5

167 ALLEGRETTO

168 ALLEGRO

169 GAILY

170 MODERATO

179 ANDANTE

mp

180 ALLEGRETTO

p

mp

181 ALLEGRETTO   Var. II of Themes and Variations, #8

mp   *mf*

p   *f*

p   *cresc.*   *f*

182 ANDANTE

mp

183 GAILY

p   *cresc.*   *mf*   *p*

184 Brightly

185 Ballando

197 Lento

Melody of Play and Sing, #23

198 Allegro con fuoco

Fine

più forte

p subito

D. C. al Fine

199 Allegretto

200 Fanfare

201 WITH A WELL-MARKED RHYTHM

202 FAST

203 PRESTO

204 ANDANTINO

FINE

D. C. AL FINE

205 MODERATO

206 PAS TROP VIF

FINE

D. C. AL FINE

207 LARGO E PESANTE

allargando

218 LÄNDLER

219 MÄSSIG UND AUSDRUCKSVOLL

220 Mesto e sostenuto

221 Allegretto, ben ritmico

222 Lively

223 Frisch

224 ANDANTE CON ESPRESSIONE

225 GIOCOSO

226 VALSE

227 LENTO

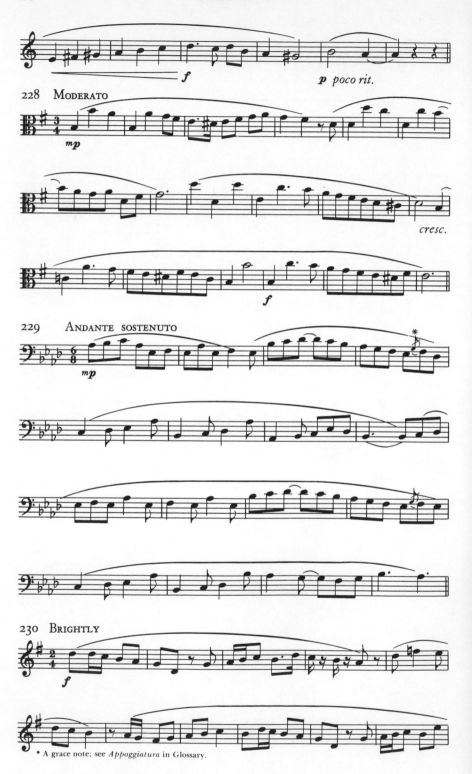

228 Moderato

229 Andante sostenuto

230 Brightly

* A grace note; see *Appoggiatura* in Glossary.

231 ANDANTE SOSTENUTO

232 MEDIUM BOUNCE

233 Moderato

234 Lively

235 Adagio espressivo e rubato

236 Quasi presto

237 Allegro non troppo

238 With dash

239 Ziemlich schnell

247 Scherzando

D. C. AL FINE

Melodies · SECTION III

Section III is to be used with Section III of all other chapters.

Chromatic alterations are used with increasing frequency in the melodies of this section. Some indicate modulation; some are factors in secondary dominant harmonies; others are melodic embellishments. Within these melodies there is an increasing diversity of rhythms, intervals, phrase structures, and musical styles. A group of modal melodies begins with #283, and modal melodies are interspersed throughout the rest of this Section.

The material of Section III can readily be correlated with the study of chromatic harmony.

Melodies · SECTION III

255 Un poco sostenuto

a tempo

256 Well accented

257 Larghetto

258 Triste mais pas trop lent

263 Modéré et gracieux

264 Allegro

265 Ländler

266 Andante maestoso　　　　Melody of Play and Sing, #44

267 ALLEGRO

268 ALLEGRETTO

269 SCHNELL UND FRÖHLICH

270 LENT ET DOUX

271 LARGHETTO

272 **Allegretto**

273 **Tempo di scherzo (in 1)**

f e staccato

274 **Lebhaft**

275 Etwas langsam und zart

276 Briskly

277 Innig

Theme of Themes and Variations, #11

Modal Melodies Based on the Following Four Modal Scales

285 ADAGIETTO (MIXOLYDIAN)

286 ANDANTE (DORIAN)

287 ANDANTE SOSTENUTO (TRANSPOSED AEOLIAN)

rall. e dim.

288 LENTO (TRANSPOSED AEOLIAN)

289 Allegretto (transposed Phrygian)

cresc.

290 Largo (Phrygian)

291 Andante (transposed Dorian)

292 Moderato (Mixolydian)

293 Allegro non troppo (transposed Mixolydian)

* * *

294   Tempo di menuetto

295   Allegro con spirito

296 So schnell wie möglich

297 Moderato

298 Valse

299 Ballando

306 ALLEGRO NON TROPPO

307 ALLEGRETTO

308 CON MOTO

313 Allegretto

314 Mässig

315 Lebhaft

316 Vif et léger

320 MEDIUM BOUNCE

321 ALLEGRETTO

322 PRESTO

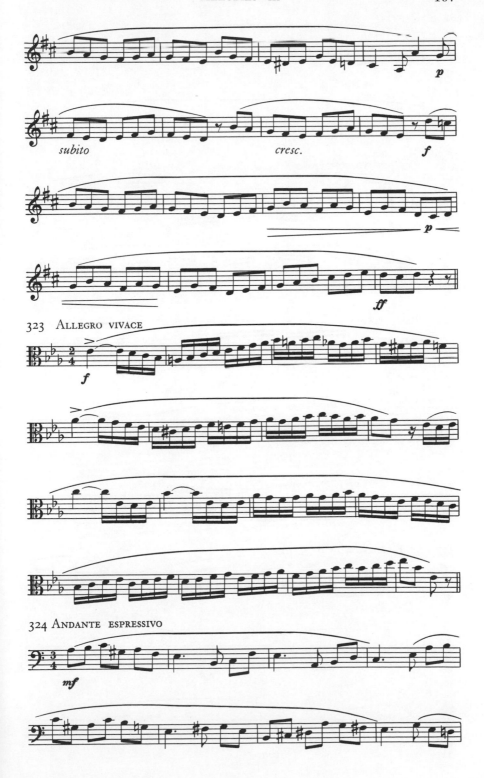

323 ALLEGRO VIVACE

324 ANDANTE ESPRESSIVO

347 ANDANTINO

348 ALLEGRETTO

349 LARGO

350 BALLANDO

a tempo

351 FAST

361 VALSE

362 LIVELY

363 ANDANTINO

364 CON MOTO

365 ETWAS LANGSAM UND ZART

366 Allegretto

367 Vif et léger

368 Allegretto

372 IN JIG TIME

373 ADAGIO APPASSIONATO

376 ANDANTE SOSTENUTO

377 EN ALLANT

382 ANDANTE, ALL'ONGARESE

383 LENTO E MESTO

384 VALSE BRILLANTE

Melodies · SECTION IV

Section IV is to be used with Section IV of all other chapters.

The melodies in this section present interesting problems of intonation, rhythm, and phrase structure. The tenor clef is introduced at the beginning of the section. Modulation to remote keys, the use of augmented and diminished intervals, a more intensified chromaticism, modal idioms, and complex syncopation offer the advanced student both challenge and stimulus.

Melodies · SECTION IV

390 **Lento**

391 **Allegro deciso**

392 **Andante**

393 **Allegretto**

394 **Presto**

395 **Minuet**

Theme of Themes and Variations, #15

416   CON CALORE

417   GALOP

cresc. al fine

418 ANDANTE   Theme of **Themes and Variations,** #17

419 VIF ET GAI

420 LARGO

421 ANDANTE E MARCATO

422 MÄSSIG UND STARK

423 ANDANTE

424 LENTO

425 ADAGIO

432 Waltz

433 Ben ritmico

434 Allegretto

cresc. poco a poco

447 ALLEGRO

448 UN POCO PESANTE

449 ANDANTE CANTABILE

452 BRISKLY

453 ANIMÉ

454 LENTO

466 Largo

467 Jolly

468 Allegro piacevole

469   VALSE TRISTE

470   ALLEGRETTO GRAZIOSO

471   ALLEGRO MODERATO

478 Allegro

493 PAS TROP VITE, MAIS AVEC FORCE

494 LEBHAFT UND STARK

im zeitmass

495 FREELY

496 ALLEGRETTO

497 LIVELY AND DETACHED

498 LENTO E ESPRESSIVO

499 Vivo

CHAPTER
TWO

Themes and Variations

Sections I, II, III, and IV are to be used with Sections I, II, III, and IV of all other chapters.

Themes and variations provide the opportunity of singing more extended musical compositions. The constantly changing character of the music as the variations unfold demands interpretive skills not required for the shorter melodies of Chapter One.

The nature of the material and the levels of difficulty are comparable to those of the melodies of Chapter One.

Themes and Variations · SECTION I

Theme and Variations, I

Theme, ANDANTE

Var. I ANDANTE

Var. II ANDANTINO

Var. III LENTO

Var. IV (Maggiore) ANDANTE

Var. V ALLEGRETTO

Theme and Variations, 2

Theme, LARGHETTO

Var. I

Var. II UN POCO ALLEGRO

Var. III Allegretto

Var. IV(Minore) Lento

Var. V(Maggiore) Allegro molto

Theme and Variations, 3

Theme Allegro moderato

Var. V Allegro con spirito

Theme and Variations, 4

Theme, Moderato

Var. I Moderato

Var. II Poco più mosso

Var. III (Minore) Largo

Var. IV (Maggiore) Allegretto

Var. V Allegro

Themes and Variations · SECTION II

Theme and Variations, 5

Var. IV(Minore) Adagietto

Var. V (Maggiore) Allegretto

Theme and Variations, 6

Theme, Lento

Var. I Un poco più mosso

Var. II Andantino

Var. III Allegretto

Var. IV (Maggiore) Adagio

Var. V (Minore) Allegro gioviale

Var. VI Allegro

Theme and Variations, 7

Theme, Moderato

Var. I Moderato

Theme and Variations, 8

Theme, ADAGIETTO

Var. I ALLA MARCIA

Var. II ALLEGRETTO

Var. III ALLEGRO MISTERIOSO

Var. IV (Maggiore) LARGO E CANTABILE

mp

mf

poco rit.

Var. V (Minore) VALSE BRILLANTE

f   *mp*

mf   *f*

p

cresc.   *mf*   *p sub.*

f   *allargando*

Theme and Variations, 9

Theme, ALLEGRETTO GIOVIALE

mf

f

Var. I Andantino

Var. II Allegro ma non troppo

Var. III Adagietto

Var. IV (Minore) Un poco agitato

Var. V(Maggiore) Allegro con brio

Themes and Variations · SECTION III
Theme and Variations, 10

Var. V Tempo di valse

Var. VI Presto

Theme and Variations, 11

Theme, Allegretto grazioso

Var. I ANDANTINO

Var. II ALLEGRO APPASSIONATO

Var. III (Maggiore) ANDANTE TRANQUILLO

Var. IV (Minore) ALLEGRETTO

Var. V Vivace

cresc. poco a poco

Theme and Variations, 13

Theme, Jolly

Var. I Fast

Theme and Variations, 14

Themes and Variations · SECTION IV

Theme and Variations, 15

Var. III (Maggiore) ALLEGRO

Theme and Variations, 16

Theme, ALLEGRETTO

Var. I ALLEGRO

Var. II ANDANTINO

Var. III (Minore) ALLEGRO

Var. IV (Maggiore) ANDANTINO CANTABILE

Var. V Allegro

Theme and Variations, 17

Theme, Andante

molto rit.

Theme and Variations, 18

Theme, ANDANTE CON MOTO

Var. I ANDANTE

Var. II ANDANTE CON MOTO

Var. III ALLEGRO

Var. IV MODERATO

CHAPTER
THREE
Duets

Sections I, II, III, and IV are to be used with Sections I, II, III, and IV of all other chapters.

The experience of singing one part while hearing another develops that sense of independence so essential to a good ensemble performer. His efforts to hear the harmonic and contrapuntal relation of his own melodic line to the other will guide the student toward maintaining correct intonation and rhythmic precision. For solo practice, it is useful to play one part at the piano while singing the other.

Duets · SECTION I

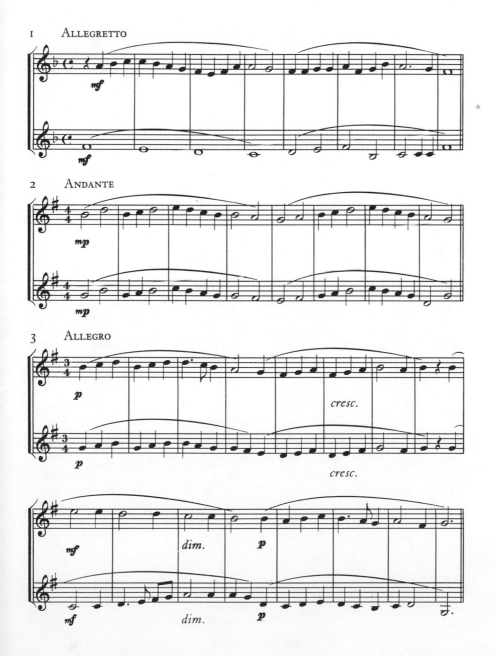

7   Allegro moderato

8   Andante con moto

12 Giocoso

13 Andantino

19   ALLEGRETTO

20   ALLEGRO

Duets · SECTION II

25   Moderato

26   Allegretto giocoso

27 ANDANTE CANTABILE

28 MODERATO

32 MODERATO ED ESPRESSIVO

33 ANDANTINO

34   Un poco sostenuto

35   Lively

36 TEMPO DI MINUETTO

Duets · SECTION III

43 ANDANTE

44 ALLEGRO

50   ALLEGRO

51   Allegretto

52 **LENTO**

53 **TEMPO DI VALSE**

54 ANDANTE

55 ANDANTINO

57 MODERATO E MARCATO

58 Adagietto

59 Spiritoso

60   DECISO

Duets · SECTION IV

63 MODERATO

64 ALLEGRO GIOCOSO

68   ANDANTE

69 Moderato e maestoso

72   ANDANTE CON MOTO

76 ANDANTE

77 ANDANTE ESPRESSIVO

78   Molto lento

CHAPTER
FOUR
Play and Sing

Sections I, II, III, and IV are to be used with Sections I, II, III, and IV of all other chapters.

These exercises are designed to provide a preparatory experience in sight singing vocal music with piano accompaniment. The piano will be especially useful to those who have difficulties with intonation.

These little pieces should be played and sung by the same person. Therefore the piano parts have been kept at a minimum level of difficulty. The emphasis is upon the melodic line and its relationship to the accompaniment. Students with little pianistic ability may use the duets of Chapter Three as additional easy play and sing exercises.

The skill acquired through the study of this chapter will allow the student to become familiar with some of the richest treasures in the musical literature. He should continue to explore all manner of music, instrumental as well as vocal.

In order to focus attention on the main purposes of these exercises, dynamics markings are not introduced until Section III.

Play and Sing · SECTION I

9   Allegretto

10   Allegro

Play and Sing · SECTION II

20 **Allegretto**

21 **Moderato**

25   ANDANTE

26   MODERATO

27   Lento

Play and Sing · SECTION III

41 ANDANTE CANTABILE

47 RECITATIVO

Play and Sing · SECTION IV

50   CON CALORE

51   TEMPO DI VALSE

55 Con calma

58 ANDANTINO

59 LARGHETTO

62 MODERATELY FAST

63 SLOW AND EXPRESSIVE

64 LARGO

65 MODERATO E MAESTOSO

66 ALLEGRO NON TROPPO

CHAPTER
FIVE

Improvisation Studies

Sections I, II, III, and IV are to be used with Sections I, II, III, and IV of all other chapters.

These exercises are intended to help the student explore the relationships of melody, harmony, and rhythm. A group of harmonic and rhythmic patterns is presented; the student must improvise a melodic line. In so doing he must of necessity give attention to the manner in which the melodic line, the underlying harmony, and the rhythmic structure combine to make up the musical whole. At the same time he must think in terms of a complete musical phrase. His creative impulse will be stimulated.

Before attempting an improvisation, the student should analyze and memorize the harmonic pattern. Next he should study the first of the rhythmic patterns listed under each chord sequence. Then he should improvise a melody using the given rhythmic pattern while accompanying himself with the harmonic sequences. He may begin by modeling his improvisation upon the illustrative examples which open each section. The melody need not be limited to chord tones; on the contrary, it can be considerably enhanced by the use of nonharmonic tones. When the student has completed the exercises which are given, he himself should invent rhythmic and harmonic patterns for further improvisation.

Improvisation Studies · SECTION I

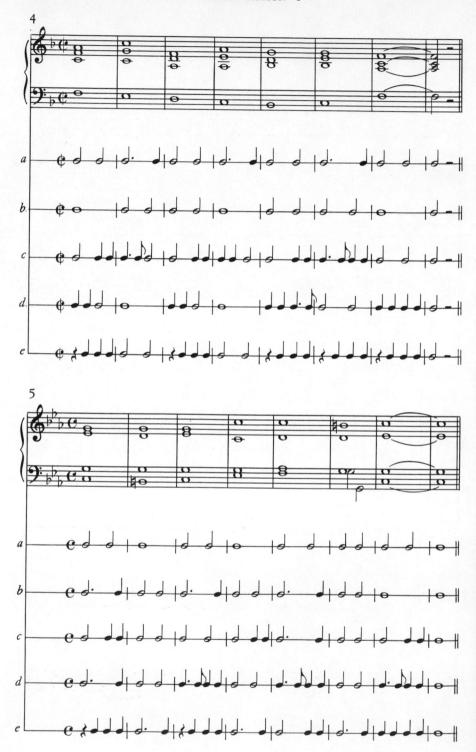

Improvisation Studies · SECTION II

Improvisation Studies · SECTION III

Improvisation Studies · SECTION IV

Supplementary Exercises

These drills are designed to focus upon various technical problems. Part I is concerned principally with problems of intonation and the development of the sense of key. Part II concentrates upon problems involving chromaticism. Both parts also contain rhythmic patterns arranged in order of increasing complexity.

Supplement · PART I

Exercises for use with Sections I and II

8

9

Exercises 10-13 are designed to show similarities and differences between the major and minor modes.

10A Major

10B   Melodic Minor

10C   Natural Minor

10D   Harmonic Minor

11A Major

11B   Melodic Minor

11 C Natural Minor

11 D Harmonic Minor

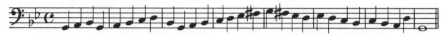

12 A

12 B

13 A

13 B

14

15

Supplement · PART II

Exercises for use with Sections III and IV

81 Ionian mode (major scale)

82 Aeolian mode (natural minor scale)

83 Harmonic minor scale

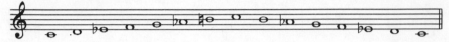

84 Melodic minor scale

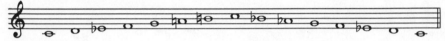

85 Dorian mode

86 Mixolydian mode

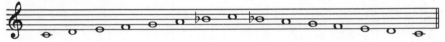

87 Phrygian mode

88 Locrian mode

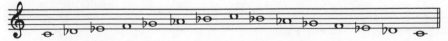

89 Lydian mode

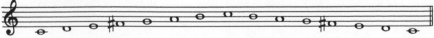

90 Whole tone scale

91 Chromatic scale

92 A

92 B

93

94

95

96

97

98

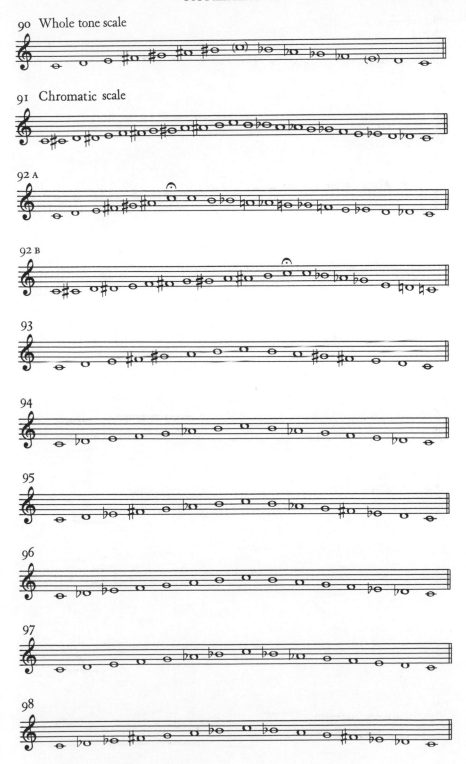

Glossary of Musical Terms

All terms are Italian unless otherwise noted.
Abbreviations are given in parentheses.

Accelerando (accel.), gradually getting faster

Adagietto, somewhat faster than adagio

Adagio, slow (slower than andante, faster than largo)

Agitato, agitated

Al fine, to the end

Alla, to the, at the, in the style of

Allargando, getting slower (crescendo often implied)

Allegretto, moderately fast (slower than allegro, faster than andante)

Allegro, fast, cheerful

All'ottavo (8 va.), at the octave

Andante, moderately slow (slower than allegretto, faster than -adagio)

Andantino, in modern usage, somewhat faster than andante; in older usage, somewhat slower than andante

Animato, animated, spirited

Animé, Fr., animated, spirited

Appassionato, impassioned, intense

Appoggiatura, a melodic ornament; of the many types there are two main classifications: the *accented (long) appoggiatura* and the *short appoggiatura* (grace note). The first, written as a small note, is accented and borrows time value from the note it precedes. The second is usually written as a small eighth or sixteenth note with a slanting stroke through the

323

hook and stem. It is executed quickly, so that the accent falls on the melody note it precedes.

Assai, very

Assez, Fr., fairly

A tempo, in the original speed

Ausdrucksvoll, Ger., expressive

Avec, Fr., with

Ben, well, very

Berceuse, Fr., lullaby

Bewegt, Ger., rather fast, agitated

Breit, Ger., broad, stately

Brillante, brilliant, sparkling

Brio, sprightliness, spirit

Calando, decreasing in both dynamics and tempo

Calmo, calm, tranquil

Calore, warmth, passion

Cantabile, in a singing or vocal style

Comodo, at a leisurely, convenient pace

Con, with

Crescendo (cresc.), increasing in volume of sound

Da capo (D. C.), from the beginning

Da capo al fine, repeat from the beginning to the end; that is, to the place where *fine* is written

Dal segno al fine, repeat from the sign to the end; that is, to the place where *fine* is written

Deciso, decisive, bold

Decrescendo (decresc.), decreasing in volume of sound

Détaché, Fr., detached

Di, of

Diminuendo (dim.), decreasing in volume of sound

Dolce, sweet (*soft* is also implied)

Doux, Fr., sweet (*soft* is also implied)

E, and
Eco, echo
Einfach, Ger., simple
En allant, Fr., moving, flowing
Espressione, expression
Et., Fr., and
Espressivo, expressive
Etwas, Ger., somewhat
Expressif, Fr., expressive

Fine, end
Force, Fr., strength, force
Forte (f), loud
Fortissimo (ff), very loud
Frisch, Ger., brisk, lively
Fröhlich, Ger., joyous, gay
Fuoco, fire

Gai, Fr., gay
Gaio, gay
Galop, Fr., a lively round-dance in duple meter
Gavotte, Fr., a French dance generally in common time, strongly
  accented, beginning on the third beat
Gedehnt, Ger., extended, sustained
Gigue, Fr., jig, a very fast dance of English origin in triple or
  sextuple meter
Giocoso, playful
Gioviale, jovial
Giusto, exact
Gracieux, Fr., graceful
Grave, very slow, solemn (generally indicates the slowest tempo)
Grazioso, graceful

Im Zeitmass, Ger., in the original speed
Innig, Ger., heartfelt, ardent

Innocente, unaffected, artless

Kräftig, Ger., strong, robust

Ländler, Ger., a country dance in triple meter
Langsam, Ger., slow
Larghetto, not as slow as largo
Largo, slow, broad
Lebhaft, Ger., lively, animated
Legato, to be performed with no interruption between tones;
    in a smooth and connected manner
Léger, Fr., light
Leggiero (also *Leggero*), light, delicate
Lent, Fr., slow
Lentement, Fr., slowly
Lento, slow; not as slow as adagio
L'istesso tempo, in the same tempo as the previous section
Lunatico, performed in the spirit of lunacy

Ma, but
Maestoso, majestic, dignified
Maggiore, major (referring to mode)
Mais, Fr., but
Marcato, marked, with emphasis
Marcia, march
Marziale, martial
Mässig, Ger., moderate
Mazurka, Polish national dance in triple meter
Meno, less
Menuetto, minuet (moderately slow dance in triple meter)
Mesto, sad, mournful
Mezzo forte (mf), moderately loud
Mezzo piano (mp), moderately soft
Minore, minor (referring to mode)
Moderato, moderate (slower than allegro, faster than andante)

Modéré, Fr., moderate (slower than allegro, faster than andante)
Molto, much, very
Mosso, in motion *(più mosso,* faster; *meno mosso,* slower)
Moto, motion
Mouvement, Fr., motion, tempo, movement

Nicht, Ger., not
Non, not

Ongarese, Hungarian

Pas, Fr., not
Pastorale, pastoral
Perdendosi, gradually fading away
Pesante, heavy, ponderous
Piano (p), soft
Pianissimo (pp), very soft
Più, more
Poco, little
Poco a poco, little by little, gradually
Pomposo, pompous
Possibile, possible
Presto, very fast (faster than allegro)

Quasi, almost, nearly

Rallentando (rall.), gradually growing slower
Rasch, Ger., fast
Recitativo, declamatory singing
Risoluto, firm, resolute
Ritardando (rit.), gradually growing slower
Ritenuto (riten.), held back
Rubato, literally, stolen; the term indicates freedom and flexibility of tempo so that the requirements of musical expression can be met

Scherzando, joking

Scherzo, jest, joke (indicating music of light, piquant character)

Schnell, Ger., fast

Sehr, Ger., very

Semplice, simple, unaffected

Sempre, always

Sforzando (sf, sfz), with force, accented

Siciliano, a moderately slow dance of pastoral character in $\frac{12}{8}$ or $\frac{6}{8}$ time

Simile, alike, in like manner

Sostenuto, sustained

Sotto voce, softly, with subdued voice

Spirito, spirit

Spiritoso, with spirit, animated

Staccato, detached

Stark, Ger., strong, vigorous

Subito (sub.), suddenly

Tanto, so much

Tempo, time; refers to rate of motion

Tempo primo (Tempo I), in the original speed

Teneramente, tenderly, delicately

Tranquillo, tranquil

Très, Fr., very

Triste, It. and Fr., sad

Trop, Fr., too much, too

Troppo, too much, too

Un, a

Und, Ger., and

Valse, Fr., waltz

Vif, Fr., lively

Vite, Fr., quickly

Vivace, lively, quick
Vivo, lively, animated

Walzer, Ger., waltz

Zart, Ger., tender, soft
Zeitmass, Ger., tempo
Ziemlich, Ger., somewhat, rather
Zu, Ger., too, to, by
Zurückhalten, Ger., to hold back, to retard

Some Frequently Used Musical Signs

\>   Accent

\<   Crescendo

\>   Diminuendo

⌢   Fermata (a hold of indeterminate length)

:‖   Repeat mark

⌢   Slur or tie

•   Staccato

—   Stressed and sustained

𝄋   Segno (sign from which repeat is made)

♩. = ♩   A tempo sign in which the first note indicates the unit of the new meter, and the second note the unit of the preceding meter. The basic pulsation in both sections is identical.